LEE, David
A Dartmoor boyhood
942.353

OTHER 'WALKING' OR 'DARTMOOR' TITLES FROM OBELISK PUBLICATIONS INCLUDE:
Diary of a Dartmoor Walker • Diary of a Devonshire Walker, *Chips Barber*
The Great Little Dartmoor Book • The Great Little Chagford Book, *Chips Barber*
Made in Devon, *Chips Barber and David FitzGerald*
Ten Family Walks on Dartmoor, *Sally and Chips Barber*
Ten Family Walks in East Devon, *Sally and Chips Barber*
Six Short Pub Walks on Dartmoor, *Sally and Chips Barber*
Ten Family Bike Rides in Devon, *Chips Barber*
Dark & Dastardly Dartmoor, *Sally and Chips Barber*
Weird & Wonderful Dartmoor, *Sally and Chips Barber*
Colourful Dartmoor • The Dartmoor Quiz Book, *Chips Barber*
Dartmoor of Yesteryear • Chagford of Yesteryear, *Chips Barber*
Walks in the Totnes Countryside, *Bob Mann* • Circular Walks on Eastern Dartmoor, *Liz Jones*
Walks in The South Hams • Pub Walks in and around The Haldon Hills, *Brian Carter*
Nine Short Pub Walks in and around Torbay, *Brian Carter*
Walks in the Shadow of Dartmoor • Walks in Tamar and Tavy Country, *Denis McCallum*
Walks in the Chagford Countryside • The A to Z of Dartmoor Tors, *Terry Bound*
The Dartmoor Mountain Bike Guide, *Peter Barnes* • The Templer Way, *Derek Beavis*
Dartmoor Letterboxing–A Beginner's Guide, *Kevin Weall*
Short Circular Walks in and around Sidmouth, *Chips Barber*
Walks on and around Woodbury Common, *Chips Barber*
Place-Names in Devon • An A–Z of Devon Dialect, *Chips Barber*
The Teign Valley of Yesteryear, Parts I and II, *Chips Barber*
Widecombe – A Visitor's Guide, *Chips Barber*
Around and About Tavistock • Around and About Roborough Down, *Chips Barber*
Along The Tavy • Along The Avon, *Chips Barber*
Railways on and around Dartmoor • Devon's Railways of Yesteryear, *Chips Barber*
Walk the East Devon Coast – Lyme Regis to Lympstone, *Chips Barber*
Walk the South Devon Coast – Dawlish Warren to Dartmouth, *Chips Barber*
Walk the South Hams Coast – Dartmouth to Salcombe, *Chips Barber*
Walk the South Hams Coast – Salcombe to Plymouth, *Chips Barber*
Okehampton Collection I, II and III, *Mike and Hilary Wreford*
Okehampton People • Okehampton of Yesteryear, *Mike and Hilary Wreford*

*We have over 200 Devon titles. For a full list of current titles please send SAE to
Obelisk Publications, 2 Church Hill, Pinhoe, Exeter EX4 9ER. Tel: (01392) 468556.*

"TO THE MEMORY OF MY MOTHER
AND OTHER MEMBERS OF MY FAMILY
WHO LOVED THE MOORS"

All photos belong to the author
apart from those on pages 5 (bottom), 12 (bottom), 13, 14 (top),
20 (top) and 28 (top) which were supplied by Chips Barber

*First published in 2004
by Obelisk Publications, 2 Church Hill, Pinhoe, Exeter, Devon, EX4 9ER
Designed and Typeset by Sally Barber
Printed in Great Britain
by Avocet Press, Cullompton, Devon*

A Dartmoor Boyhood

Introduction

Had it not been for the threatened outbreak of war in 1939, my parents would not have returned to Devon, my life would almost certainly have been different, and there would have been none of these 'Dartmoor Boyhood' memories to recount with such affection.

Ernest A. Chown, my maternal grandfather, developed a great love for Dartmoor in the early 1900s and camped many times beside the Doetor Brook, near Lydford. Some of his pictures have been included in this book. Sometimes this was with friends or other members of the family, including his wife Marian (known as 'Minnie' and shown here), his only daughter and elder child Doreen (who was my mother), and his only son Cyril.

One August, about 1918, my grandfather sent a postcard to my mother at Exmouth. It read: *Catch the 7.52, not 8.25 train. Bring your Serge Dress, also boots, leather shoes for running about round the camp. Plenty of Moss here; can't dry it. Lovely spot in a Glen 50 yards below bridge is our pitch. Bring thick stocking. Fond love from Dad.* Mother caught the through train from Exmouth and alighted at Bridestowe station, the one at Lydford being a mile and a half beyond the village at the bottom of the Gorge.

As he got older, grandfather wanted something more substantial than a tent in which to spend his holidays: akin to camping but with a few more creature comforts. So he got permission from farmer William Kennard, of Downtown Farm, to put the Cabin in one of his fields. This was in the early 1920s, before planning permission had come in. Nowadays such a structure would never be allowed, particularly within the Dartmoor National Park. It was in this setting that the earlier part of the events recalled in these pages took place.

In reading through them please remember that they portray the world as seen through the eyes of a small child: I was scarcely four years old when we first went to live at Lydford, and only seven when we returned to live permanently in Exmouth in 1944.

Camping beside the Doetor Brook

The Setting

The moor is a strange place – some call it 'the last wilderness'. Its effect always seems to be positive: either one hates the sight of it, or else it calls forth a strange kind of love. Once enfolded in this love there is no escape – only death can bring release. Its chains bind for ever the hearts of those who love it. My mother, her parents and her brother all loved the moor, but my father never cared for it and would visit only reluctantly.

Downtown Farm stretched from the main line of the Southern Railway, running between Lydford and Bridestowe, to the very edge of the moor. Its land gradually rose up towards the east with the highest part just above one thousand feet. Its farm lands were bisected by the main road from Okehampton to Tavistock; in the roadside hedge of one of the fields was the milestone that showed us we were exactly 8 miles from each. At the edge of the enclosed land, at High Down, the open moor began. The land then sloped to the valley of the River Lyd where there is a ford and a footbridge, known as the Fording Bridge. A short way downstream is Black Rock, a large outcrop of metamorphic rock, below which is a natural swimming pool.

Beyond, and to the east of the river, the moor rises more steeply with two tors masking the view in this direction: Arms Tor to the left, Bray Tor to the right. Incidentally, we always knew this rocky eminence as Bray Tor because this is how it was named on all the postcards, published by Chapmans, which one could then buy at Lydford Post Office. The spelling 'Brat Tor' on the Ordnance Survey map is wrong. William Crossing (1847–1928) called it Bra Tor, whilst the late Eric Hemery, another Dartmoor author, referred to it as Brai Tor, but, regardless of spellings, they are pronounced the same way!

On the top of Bray Tor stands a landmark: a cross about thirteen feet high. It was erected to mark the Golden Jubilee of Queen Victoria in 1887 by William Widgery (1826–1893), a Dartmoor artist who lived in Lydford village (in what later became the Lydford House Hotel). South-eastwards of Widgery Cross is Doe Tor, separated from it by the Doetor Brook (or as we knew it, the River Doe). Behind this range of three tors lies another run of outcrops, with Sharp Tor and Hare Tor closing the view in that direction.

Looking from 'Bray Tor' towards Hare Tor

The village of Lydford lay about a mile westward of our Cabin field, but much of our view in that direction was shut off by the high ground of Burley Down and Beara Down. There was a quarry on the side of Burley Down, which showed as a white gash on the hillside.

This area of Dartmoor is unique in that the streams run parallel to the moor instead of flowing more or less straight out from it. The River Lyd runs between the granite of Dartmoor to its east and the altered slatey rocks (the 'metamorphic aureole') to its west. Behind and to the east of the Lyd is the Doetor Brook; still further to the east is the Rattlebrook, which falls into the Tavy. It is this configuration which gives the area its uniqueness, with three ranges of tors and hills lying one behind the other. Just beyond the Rattlebrook is the long downward sweep of Amicombe Hill, which falls from the heights of Kitty Tor towards Watern Oke.

The Cabin

This stood by itself in a field on the edge of Dartmoor; all that lay between it and the open moor was a narrow field. The farther hedge was of the 'corn ditch' type (a vertical stone wall behind an outer ditch) and the moor began beyond it, rolling eastwards for many unpopulated miles until descending at length to where human habitation began again.

Originally it was just a single bedroom hut with a lean-to behind to serve as the kitchen, but after a time the second hut was attached. This was how it was when my mother, sister Diana and I lived there during the 1939–1945 war. The additional kitchen hut had been brought down by train from Exmouth to Bridestowe station and from there it was transported to the field on Mr Kennard's farm cart. The Cabin was effectively two large beach huts – a kitchen and a bedroom – joined together by a narrow lobby. Each hut also had an outside door; as the field sloped gently westwards, the front was some two feet above the ground. Inside, the walls were panelled with lightly varnished plywood, whilst the outside of the front of the bedroom hut was shingled, as was the roof. The remainder of the exterior was tarred or creosoted.

One wall of the kitchen was about six feet away from the hedge, in which was a large tree partly overhanging the roof. On the outside of the side wall nearest the hedge was a meat safe made of wood and zinc gauze, but sufficiently high above the ground to be out of reach of any sheep, cattle or ponies that might have been in the field. The Cabin stood unprotected and often the sheep would rub themselves against its corners. When it was first erected, mushrooms used to grow in the grass at the back of the kitchen.

In the bedroom there were two beds, the frames of which were made from heavy duty, silver-painted iron piping. Stretched across each frame was a piece of stout canvas (probably sailcloth). The canvas was kept taut and in position by ropes passed through the ring holes and around the pipe frame. A mattress and bedding were put on top of the canvas. There was just sufficient room between the two beds for a narrow camp bed if needed. Space was sometimes at a premium.

The Cabin stood by the short southerly hedge, sideways on with the front facing west. It was about halfway up the side of a field that was oblong in shape and rose steadily towards the moor from the gate at the lowest corner. From this gate a beautiful lane led down to the main road. By Dartmoor standards it was a big field – about ten acres. At that time the trees and bushes on top of the hedges were so high they effectively cut off all sight of the nearest houses: some three fields away, stretched out along the main road. I cannot remember the hedges ever being layered. Thus the Cabin was isolated.

The soil in the field was very stony and of no great depth, so it was never ploughed, but it was usually stocked with sheep, or occasionally ponies, so that the grass was always well cropped. At the bottom of the field was our water supply – a spring of cold, crystal-clear water. It came out of a piece of earthenware pipe and fell into a small pool, running on down

Mother, Diana and me beneath 'Bray Tor'

by the bottom hedge and out of the field by the gate. This was amongst a riot of water plants including marsh buttercups and forget-me-nots. Just outside the field gate it was joined by the water from another spring, which rose in the adjacent field. Our spring had never been known to fail, even in severe drought. My grandfather used to say that when there was a drought, and the village wells dried up, the people would come to this spring for water.

Across the little pool was a plank on which one stood to stoop down when filling up the water jug. The system was always the same – one filled a large metal container holding, perhaps, a gallon and a half, by first catching the water coming out of the pipe in a small jug and then decanting this into the large container. We were always most particular to see that only water which had come out of the pipe went into the jug. If you caught up water from the pool, you were liable to bring up small black creatures with it, little bigger than a pin head. On one occasion I remember a visitor offering to fetch the water and coming back up with it very quickly. Of course she had scooped the water out of the pool; it all had to be thrown away and a fresh supply fetched. One was always careful with water, as every drop had to be fetched and carried about a hundred yards from the spring to the Cabin. Water is heavy. In later years, when staying at the Cabin, one always noticed the difference between having a ready supply of tap water at home and one's attitude to it when it had to be fetched from the spring, especially in heavy rain!

The water pipe

If you jumped across the brooklet and went through a gate into the next field you would find our lavatory, or privy. This was a small galvanised iron shed in the triangular corner of the field, almost hidden by the tall trees in the hedge tops leaning over it. It was of the earth closet type; one of Mother's weekly chores was the digging of a pit. This was a particularly arduous task as the earth was stony. The smell from the contents of the bucket as they vanished into the pit had to be experienced to be believed, though usually it was dosed with Harpic or something similar. We thought nothing of it; it was a task familiar to thousands of country people in the days before the advent of public sewerage systems. That particular part of the field must have become very fertile! At any rate, very luxuriant docks grew there.

It was in the summer of 1941 that we three first went to live in the Cabin. Prior to that we had lived in Exmouth, but went to the Cabin because of the bombing of the town by German planes returning from attacks on Exeter. At that time I was four and my sister Diana was two and a half. Because of its isolation, we never slept at the Cabin; just lived in it during the day. In the evening we used to walk down the lane, cross the main road, and go down another lane to the farmhouse where we slept.

Downtown House was very old, with little more in the way of modern amenities than the Cabin. The back part of the house seemed to be the oldest and it looked as though it had been doubled in size at some time by building on another part along the whole of one side. I remember there were two roofs like a W turned upside down. The newer part contained the front door, with a small garden in front of that, but it was in fact never used as an entrance to the house. There was no internal water supply, only a spring outside the back door. This fell into a large granite trough with internal dimensions about the size of a modern bath. The whole was housed in a stone-built three-sided shed open on the house side.

As the ground on which the house was built rose up slightly, both it and the water supply shed were on a slightly higher level than the farmyard; a series of shallow steps led up to the back door.

The risers were formed from stones cleared, no doubt, from the fields; each step was cobbled with further stones set on edge into the earth. At any time of the year, anyone who fancied a bath must have been very hardy to face the ice cold water in the granite trough. Maybe, like Queen Elizabeth I, they only took a bath once every three months whether they needed one or not! More likely the residents never indulged in such 'dangerous modern practices'.

Downtown, near Lydford

The farmhouse always had its own attractive aroma, which perhaps came from home-baked bread. The cooking facilities were basic. The Kennards did not even have a range but cooked over the fire in the large kitchen hearth, with crocks hanging down suspended from the chimney. The bread oven was to one side.

Like the Cabin, the house had no electricity for lighting: nothing but candles and oil lamps. Being a rural area, gas was not available. Houses down in the village had electricity, but the farmhouse was a little off the beaten track and I don't

Downtown

suppose the Kennards, being true Dartmoor farmers of the real old-fashioned type, would have held with such newfangled notions, let alone parted with the cash to have electricity brought in.

I remember the white-painted doors of the bedrooms, with latches instead of locks and handles, and the small windows in thick stone walls. As with most small children, we did not like to go to sleep in the dark, so we used a night light. At first this consisted of a china container filled with cottonwool soaked in paraffin, with a small wick protruding through a hole in the top, but later it was replaced by a small paraffin lamp with an opaque shade. We called both our night lights 'Tinkerbell' (from *Peter Pan*) and were very fond of them. I slept on a canvas camp bed that had been brought down from the Cabin. Mother, Diana and I all slept in the same bedroom, but Mother would of course sit downstairs with the family until it was time for her to go to bed.

Particularly memorable was the walk each day to and from the farmhouse. We each had a walking stick, which we used to ride between our legs rather like a hobby horse. Mine was called Dobbin. When we reached the farmhouse in the evening we left our 'horses' overnight in the porch outside the back door; in the morning we remounted them for the ride up the lanes to the Cabin.

The little brooklet that began with the spring in our field ran down in a shallow ditch at the side of the lane leading from the Cabin to the main road. On the other side of this lane, the hedge top consisted largely of hazel trees from which we used to gather nuts in the autumn. Between the cart track and the brooklet grew a large number of gorse bushes. Spiders were prolific here and it was always a revelation to walk up the lane on a sunny morning and see the masses of dew diamonds glittering in the sun on the spiders' webs; it was incredibly beautiful. Yes, such a simple thing, yet the memory is precious and one that the passing years have done nothing to dim. My mother felt exactly the same way and would also recall those dew diamonds years afterwards.

Each of the two rooms in the Cabin was small – no more than eight feet by ten feet – so when it was wet we had to stay indoors where there was very little room to play. With the doors shut and the Primus and oil stove going, it very quickly became warm. There were no carpets on the floor, but they were covered by linoleum with coconut matting on top of that.

Being in a field with sheep and sometimes horses, naturally at times we were troubled with flies. Mother once bought a roll of sticky flypaper in the village and hung it from one of the beams in the bedroom. Unfortunately, it was either not tied up firmly enough or else too low, but the inevitable happened: the flypaper and Mother's hair somehow merged. Once that had happened nothing would persuade them to part; like a limpet they clung together. What a touching sight: demonstrable proof of the effectiveness of flypaper. Eventually the flypaper and part of Mother's hair had to be cut off with a pair of scissors. Mother's remarks on this occasion are not recorded!

At the farmhouse they had a radio that ran off an accumulator. After we had gone to bed, Mother would sit with Mr and Mrs Kennard and their unmarried son and daughter, Tom and Bessie. They all spoke the very broadest Devon dialect with a rather harsh nasal sound, which seems peculiar to the Dartmoor country. In other parts of the county, the dialect is softer. How I wish it had been possible to record their voices. What the grownups talked about, I do not know, but guess it must have been the progress of the war, the state of the crops, and probably the doings of the locals and the 'furriners' who had come to the village to escape the bombing of the cities and towns.

I am told that on one occasion, as I was sitting next to Mother on the settee at Downtown, I turned to her and, for no apparent reason whatsoever, bit her firmly and surely on the bottom. I cannot recall either the event or the outcome, but was probably sent straight to bed. Luckily Mother did not develop rabies! We rarely saw Father, as he was serving in the RAF.

Pastimes and Walks

It would be foolish to pretend that we had an intimate knowledge of the moor at this time, because we did not. We were only very small and so not capable of walking great distances.

Great Links Tor

Besides, Dartmoor was requisitioned for military training during the war and so was out of bounds. However, we did become intimately acquainted with a small part of it in our immediate neighbourhood. This comprised the small area from Great Nodden (which we knew as Bull Hill) in the north to Doe Tor in the south, and from High Down in the west to the valley of the River Doe and Dick's Well Pits in the east. We never climbed to the top of Great Links Tor, nor did we get as far as either Bleak House in the Rattlebrook valley or Tavy Cleave. Mother often used to talk about these places and we wanted to see them. Tavy Cleave would have been difficult to access because of the firing ranges at Willsworthy, and Bleak House too would have been within the danger area of the central Okehampton ranges. We used to ply

Crossing the Tavy at Rattlebrook Foot

Mother with questions about Bleak House. How much of it was really left? Had it got floors in it and windows? Had it got a staircase? We knew, of course, that it had long been abandoned, and that it had been built for an employee of the Rattlebrook Peat Works, miles from any other dwelling. But generally we seemed to be dissatisfied with her answers, which probably were rather vague. The only satisfactory answer would have been to see it for ourselves, but that was impossible then. Thus it remained a distant enigma, yearned for, but not realised, and I was well into my teens before I saw it for the first time. Nowadays there is not much of it left, but when I first saw it, in about 1953, the front walls were still intact up to roof-plate level, with four gaping holes where the windows had been. The central cross dividing wall, with fireplaces on both sides and the chimney stack above, was also in place, but fell many years ago.

Bleak House

Lydford Gorge

Much the same sort of feelings applied to Tavy Cleave and also Lydford Gorge. Because of the war, the Gorge was closed, though a few of the more adventurous spirits from the village had got down into it. We used to hear about the whirlpool down in its depths – the Devil's Cauldron it is called, a name surely to awaken any child's curiosity. Grandmother had told us that when she visited it as a young bride, she was too terrified to walk out over the plank to look into its murky depths. So it remained something to conjure with: a name suggesting mystery.

It was in the early 1950s that I first got to visit Tavy Cleave, which surely is the most dramatic valley anywhere on Dartmoor. On one side you have the great beetling cliffs surmounted by the Tavy Cleave Tors, of which Tavy Cleave Sharp is definitely the most dramatic, rising as it does from the valley floor in what must be about the steepest hillside of the moor. In the centre rushes the River Tavy, reputed to be the second fastest-flowing river in the British Isles, and on the

Looking down the Lyd valley towards Brentor

A Dartmoor Boyhood

further (south) side, the valley rises fairly steeply, strewn with rocks, though not so thickly as on the other side. As children we had an idea of what part of the Cleave looked like; in the office of his shop at Exmouth, grandfather had a photo showing the lower bathing pool. He had taken this photo himself many years before. Mother had read to us Charles Kingsley's story *The Water Babies*, and when I first saw the Cleave from the cleft beside Tavy Cleave Sharp Tor, I always imagined that it was a valley something like this in which Tom, the boy chimney sweep, had climbed down in order to bathe in the river. I was also put in mind of a couple of lines from Tennyson's poem 'The Passing of Arthur' from *The Idylls of the King*, which we learnt at Grammar School as an excellent example of onomatopoeia: *Dry clashed his harness in the barren caves And icy chasms, and all to left and right The bare black cliff clanged round him.*

To walk out to the River Lyd was easy; it was not very far. From the Cabin all one had to do was walk up to a gap in the hedge, cross another narrow field, go through another gap in the top hedge and into the Newtake, which at that time was indistinguishable from the open moor. From Moor View there was a very well-used footpath through Vale Down, which also gave access to the Newtake, via a couple of upright stones set just far enough apart to allow a human (but not a sheep!) to squeeze through. Once through, a broad green path through luxuriant heather continued across the Newtake leading to a gate on to High Down. Nowadays the gate is padlocked and has been replaced by a stile over the wall. Almost always one would meet other people on this path, or, if not people, then one would frequently see different sorts of butterflies, and plenty of slugs if the weather was damp. Many gorse bushes grew on the western side of the path through Vale Down, which ran very close to the northern boundary of Farmer Kennard's fields. Also growing in the high hedge bank, in season, were plenty of blackberries; this was a good spot to pick them. Within its limits we got to know the Lyd valley very well.

At Black Rock the bathing pool had a rock protruding from the bottom of it; the American soldiers encamped at Bridestowe talked about blasting it out with dynamite to improve and deepen the pool for diving and swimming. At some stage since our time at Lydford, this rock has in fact gone from the pool. Most of the river flows over a low waterfall between two large rocks on either side, and this is where the pool is at its deepest. Although Black Rock is not named on the Ordnance Survey Map, it is rather a special place, beloved of many people. On the west side, the rocks rise up sheer in two places, both of which have a seat at their foot. The place has poignant memories for some, and in most years a poppy wreath is placed there, beneath the memorial tablet to Captain Nigel Hunter, who was killed in action in March 1918 at the age of 23. The poem he wrote on his last visit to this area sums up the whole feeling of the place:

Are we not like this Moorland Stream,
Springing none knows where from;
Twinkling, Bubbling flashing agleam
Back at the Sun: ere long
Gloomy and dull, under a cloud,
Then rushing onwards again,
Dashing at rocks with anger loud,
Roaring and foaming in vain.
Wandering thus for many a mile,
Twisting and turning, away for a while;
Then of a sudden 'tis over the fall,
And the dark still pool is the end of all.

Is it? I thought, as I turned away,
And I turned again to the silent moor.
Is it? I said and my heart said "nay"
As I gazed at the Cross on Widgery Tor.

As you stand at the seat, having read the poem, there below you is the 'dark still pool' and the little waterfall, whilst if you raise your eyes you will behold the granite cross (Widgery Cross) on the highest rock of Bray Tor.

Black Rock

We knew all the shallow pools and falls on other parts of the river, such as the overflow from the intake works on the Doe, which ran out by the Telegraph Bridge over the Lyd. (The Telegraph Bridge was so called because it was made of several old telegraph poles laid side by side.) It gave foot access to Doetor Farm, which was then inhabited. The bridge has completely vanished and the farmhouse is now a heap of rubble. Vehicular access was by either High Down Ford or Mary Emma Ford, which was beside the Telegraph Bridge.

We knew the two old quarries further up the Lyd where the troops used to practise with rifles; the pipe across the bed of the river bringing down the water supply for Bridestowe from a spring, enclosed within a wire fence, on the side of Arms Tor; the stone enclosure near Black Rock, where a spring was piped to give a water supply to Lydford, and we could walk around the flat-topped walls, being especially careful as we went up the steep part where it climbed the bank, and even more careful as it came down again on the other side – wild white raspberries grew inside it; the little gravelly beach beside the Fording Bridge; the tiny island in midstream not far below; and many other delightful spots.

There was a boy who said he could tickle trout. We watched him plunge his hand into the stream, moving gently towards the submerged undersides of the boulders in the stream bed where the trout lurked. Whether it was an idle boast, or whether he really could catch trout in this way, I do not know. At any rate, he never caught any when we watched him. I seem to remember that he was the son of PC Seldon, the village bobby.

One of Grandfather's camps

14

Breaking camp

How High Down has changed! Then it was covered with luxuriant heather; now all that has completely gone and there is little but grass and gorse, though here and there a little heather seems to be coming back. This was still the time when walkers would come for a week or fortnight's holiday, staying at local guest houses. The high numbers of cars which one gets at High Down nowadays just did not exist then. It was our little world and we loved it. To small children it seemed quite a large area, but through adult eyes it is not, of course, very large. We were good walkers (well, we had to be – the only form of transport was either a pram or Mother's bicycle), but with wartime restrictions and difficulties there was little alternative anyway. Sometimes, however, we would catch the bus into either Tavistock or Okehampton, generally for extra shopping, but occasionally for a little excursion to Grenofen, on the other side of Tavistock.

Another place that we often wondered about was Cranmere Pool; Mother used to tell us about her visit to it in thick mist when she was taken there by her parents. Grandmother was also fond of recalling their experiences on that occasion: how they got lost and thoroughly wet through. To young ears, it all sounded very exciting and daring. This, of course, had happened years before we were born, when Mother and her brother were teenagers and their parents were camping in tents on the moor.

Apart from my pretend horse Dobbin, we sometimes used to borrow a real horse from Tom Kennard, the farmer. Blackbird, as his name implies, was black all over; he was very docile and well over twenty at this time, but there was still life left in him and he lived on into his thirties. We would ride on Blackbird's back part of the time if we went out onto the moor, and this was a help in getting small reluctant feet up some of the steeper ascents. In this manner I first climbed to Widgery Cross. The path invariably taken at that time was one that led up to the col between Arms Tor and Bray Tor, though nowadays people take a much steeper, more direct path to the summit. On the southern side of this hill is a rock which, when seen from the valley below, looks very much like a sheep, but, unlike the rock in the Lyd at Black Rock, this one is still there!

Playing in the Lyd

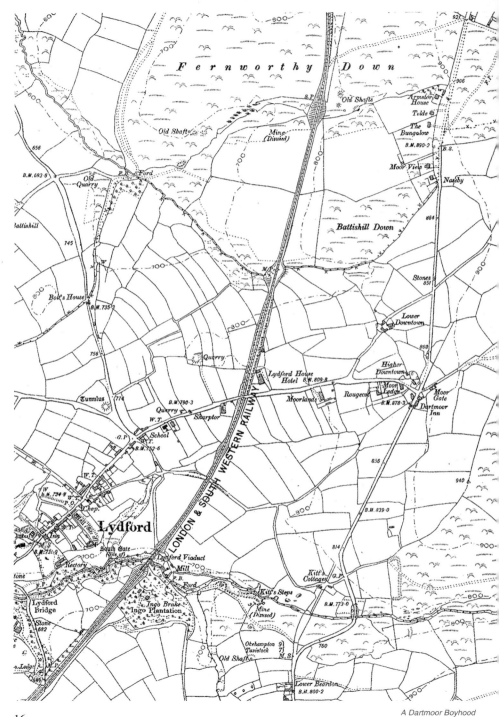

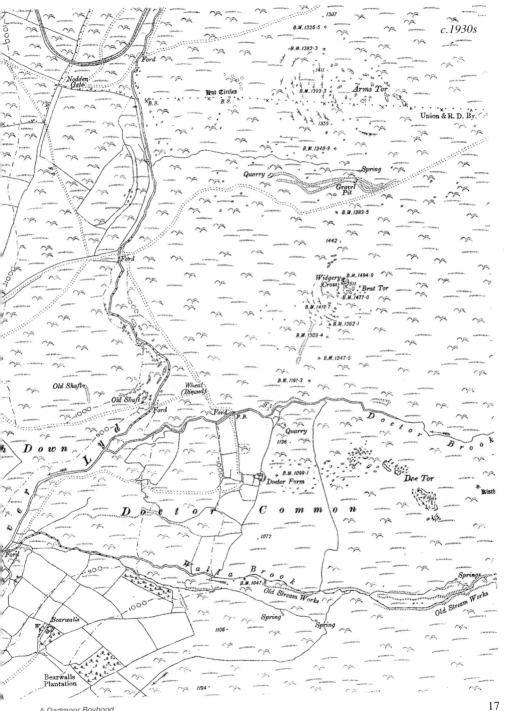

c.1930s

By virtue of its high rainfall, Dartmoor is a place of running water and one can never be far from the sound of its many streams. We spent hours playing by the spring in our field and we frequently went to various favourite spots on the River Lyd. Apart from bathing when it was warm enough, we would build dams and sail paper boats or small rafts woven from the rushes, which grew in many places by the stream. When we were at school we used to sing the line from 'All Things Bright and Beautiful' which talks about *The meadows where we play, the rushes by the water we gather every day.* These words always lived for me because it was real within my experience, although admittedly not as a daily occurrence. The paper boats were made by folding paper in a certain way into a gradually reducing triangular shape and then pulling out the ends – a form of origami. They never floated for long because the paper quickly became sodden. Sometimes we would

build 'houses' by piling the flatter stones from the riverbed one on top of the other in a form of tower. Often we would take our tea with us and this meant making a fireplace in some sheltered spot, or else using one previously made by other visitors. These were generally built in a horseshoe-shape, using flattish stones from the riverbed, which were of just sufficient width to allow a kettle to rest across the top without actually falling down into the fire. Quite often it was necessary to build only two side walls as the back could be formed by using an earthbound

boulder. Generally one lit the fire first, allowed it to burn a bit and for charcoal to form before putting the kettle on it. We took a large brown one with us, which we filled from the stream and then boiled to make tea. If we were near the Lydford water supply enclosure, then we would fill the kettle from its overflow, which was probably rather cleaner than the river water, although we never suffered any harm from drinking it.

With many years of use for the open-air boiling of water, the sides of the kettle had grown black. The fire was made by burning dry heather twigs, which were abundant, and what an aromatic scent they gave off as they burned! A plug of newspaper was put in the spout of the kettle to keep out the smoke and any flying embers from the fire. Tea leaves and cups had to be taken out in a basket as well. One never sees these little fireplaces now: it's illegal to light fires.

A Dartmoor Boyhood

During our time at the Cabin we spent only the summers there; our permanent home was in Exmouth. We would go down perhaps in May, and the latest we stayed was well into October. Both my sister and I were under school age at this time, so there was no problem in this respect. We had few toys with us and this I suppose was why we sometimes used to think of home – not that we had that many in Exmouth either. With the streams and long summer days (Double Summer Time) their absence was not something which we minded. The natural world gave ample scope and I can never remember saying, "I'm bored!" We just did not need artificial props for our amusement.

Letters and milk were delivered to a special box concealed on top of the hedge, just inside the gate at the bottom of the Cabin lane; we collected the milk each day as we walked back to the Cabin up the lane from Downtown. All our other provisions had to be brought by hand from Lydford village, about a mile away. Mother took the pushchair to pile the groceries in and also to carry the essential paraffin can and meths bottle. The pram was certainly necessary for the return journey, as it was uphill all the way home.

There was a right of way to the village through the lanes leading to Downtown Farm, and this cut off a corner and a steepish hill. Old Farmer Kennard was very jealous to limit this to a foot right of way only. Whilst he allowed us to walk through with the pram, other people were challenged. I well remember him shouting at two newcomers to the district who pushed prams through his farmyard. I seem to recollect that he let them continue their journey, but warned them not to come that way again if they were going to bring prams with them. Generally there was a furious barking of dogs when anybody walked through the farmyard. These dogs were rarely seen as they were kept shut up in a windowless shed near the path. I doubt if they were very well cared for, although they were almost certainly sheepdogs.

In the village, apart from the Post Office which incorporated a general stores, there were a butcher's shop (Hannafords, pronounced 'Annavurds' by the locals), two more general stores and one that sold clothes. There was also a cobbler called Mr Cook, who I think did this work part-time, as I seem to remember that he also worked at Meldon Quarry. After the war he and his wife opened a guest house, called Kirtonia, on Vale Down. We stayed there once when Moor View was full.

The paraffin and meths were purchased in the village at the garage which has now gone. The Post Office and general stores was kept by Miss Petherick, although the actual Post Office section was run by Miss Cummings. She, I recollect through childish eyes, seemed very old. She wore spectacles, her hair in a bun, and was very prim and proper, although she possessed a sweet disposition. Miss Petherick was also a kindly soul and saw to the general stores side of the business. We did most of our shopping there, but sometimes used the other general store, which was just a small, square single-storey brick building a bit further up the village from the Post Office. No trace of this building remains. Very occasionally we might go into Tavistock by bus for a bit of shopping, or, more rarely still, go to Okehampton. Sadly, there is now no Post Office nor any shop at all in the village; the Post Office is contained in the garage shop close to the Dartmoor Inn.

I can vividly recollect sitting in the Cabin during a tremendous thunderstorm raging directly overhead. Mother used to tell us that the bangs and rumbles were caused by a giant in the sky tipping coal into his coal cellar. Incidentally, clotted cream and golden syrup spread thickly on bread is known as thunder and lightning. Normally cream was unobtainable because of wartime restrictions, but we were able to get it from the Kennards, who made their own. Unfortunately it was wasted on Diana and me as we did not like it then. Nor did we care for cheese. I have a faint recollection of going into the dairy at Downtown Farm and seeing the great bowls with the gently heated milk in them and the thick crust of clotted cream on the top.

Maybe people did not bathe at the farm in the granite trough, but we used to have baths at the Cabin. When the time came, Mother would take a galvanised wash tub from its store under the Cabin and stand it on the table in the kitchen hut. Water heated on the oil stove and Primus was then poured in and there was just room for a child to get in with their legs drawn up to the chin. We would both be bathed in the same water. During the wartime rationing, people living in this part of the county were fortunate because the water off the moor was extremely soft and one hardly needed to use any soap or washing powder. In fact, we used to send some of our spare soap to our Grandmother Lee, who lived outside London where the water was very hard.

The versatile kitchen table was also used for ironing clothes on. As there was no electricity, this had to be done with a flat iron, which was stored in a metal container with a clip to keep the iron in place. When ironing was necessary, Mother would light the Primus stove and place the flat iron on top of it to heat up, a process which had to be repeated from time to time as the iron began to cool.

We did not always go to the moor for our walks. Sometimes we would go in the opposite direction, down to the village, turning right at the War Memorial Cross, and then walk through the lanes either as far as the foot of Galford Down and back the same way, or more often to Watergate at the foot of Burley Down. At other times we might go to the village via Kitt's (or Skitt's) Steps, which is a waterfall higher up the River Lyd than the commencement of the Gorge. In Dartmoor books written in the early nineteenth century, Kitt's Steps is generally portrayed as being superior to the White Lady waterfall at the bottom of the Gorge. In her book *Home Scenes*, published in 1846, Rachel Evans says that this cascade is spoilt by the near vicinity of a working mine. By our time this had long since ceased to work, but below the fall was an excavation (possibly an old adit), which was used as a dumping place for unwanted rubbish. I vividly recall that we were fascinated by a metal artificial leg, which lay amongst the discarded items.

THE TOP of KITTS STEPS. LYDFORD 12594

The Doctor Brook

When the whortleberries were in season, in July and August, we would go up the River Doe (Doetor Brook) to pick the fruit from the side of Doe Tor. This was a good spot for worts (the Devonshire name for whortleberries) as there was always a good plentiful crop there. Whilst the plants are still there, the abundance of fruit on them seems to be something that has vanished. The worts would be either stewed and eaten with custard or perhaps cream, or else made into jelly or a pie. It was always obvious if you had eaten worts because your teeth and tongue would be stained purple. Nowadays few people bother to pick as it is a slow, backbreaking process and it takes quite a long time to gather a reasonable quantity.

Mention earlier in this section of the bathing pool at Black Rock prompts the recollection that in August 1952, at the time of the Lynmouth flood disaster, we were staying for our summer holiday at Moor View on the main road. Although Dartmoor did not have quite the deluge that fell on Exmoor, nevertheless it certainly received a very substantial amount of rain. We walked out to look at the River Lyd, which was coming down in a roaring brown torrent. Although I have seen it in spate on several occasions since then, I have never seen it so high as it was that day. At Black Rock there are two large high rocks standing in the bed of the stream and normally most of the river flows between these and over a low waterfall into the pool. Such was the volume of water on this occasion, however, that it was pouring over the top of the left-hand rock (the one which is immediately under the memorial plaque to Capt Nigel Hunter) and was almost over the top of the right-hand one, which is slightly higher. Every other smaller rock in the stream bed was completely covered and the river had burst its banks. Somewhat further upstream there was a man fishing, but I should think it is doubtful whether he caught anything.

Vale Down

The time came when Mother decided that we must forsake the Cabin. I think this was because I was five years old and therefore must start attending the village school. We looked at several properties for rent before settling for two rooms in a large guest house on Vale Down. This was only about a quarter of a mile away from the Cabin.

Vale Down is the stretch of road which lies on the main Okehampton to Tavistock road between the Fox and Hounds Inn, at the head of the road leading down to Bridestowe, and the Dartmoor Inn, opposite the road leading down to Lydford.

Moor View

Moor View was a large double-fronted detached house with big rooms. It was built of the local rusty-coloured stone. Corners and surrounds to doors and windows were of brick. I sometimes wonder if the stone came from one of the two small quarries beside the River Lyd on the slopes leading up to Great Nodden. We had a large sitting room on the left-hand side at the front of Moor View, and a bedroom on the side at first floor level. Altogether there were six bedrooms and a boxroom. Downstairs there were three large reception rooms, a back sitting room and a large kitchen.

Moor View was run by Miss Doris Crocker, whom we called Aunty Doris. I can remember the three of us going there for the first time when Mother enquired if rooms were available. During the period that we lived there, we spent one winter on the moor. Mother brought the paraffin cooker with us from the Cabin so that she could do her own cooking. The house itself, in its large kitchen, had a temperamental, old-fashioned, black-leaded range. Aunty Doris was always cross when it went out, as it was not very easy to light. Usually there was a large black kettle on top of the range. Doris and her mother used the back sitting room, as it was smaller than the other three.

I shall always associate mutton with our stay at Lydford. It was, naturally, the sheep off the moor which provided the only fresh meat obtainable from the butcher. It was decidedly mutton, not lamb, and I cannot say that I cared much for it, especially when eaten cold. There was also the other wartime meat, corned beef. Very occasionally we would have delicious Spam, or sometimes rabbit stew, the rabbit being the gift of Tom Kennard, on whose land the Cabin stood. Rabbits were more common then and their burrows were in the hedges of the fields. At that time he used to catch them in a gin, a cruel trap which is now illegal.

Moor View also had several fields of its own behind it, extending to about 60 acres. At the back and to one side of the house were various sheds. In one of them Doris kept her car, an Austin Seven. At the back was a barn with cattle stalls below and a hay loft above. These were built mainly of wood and corrugated iron. Stored in them were various bits of old broken furniture, which had been thrown out from the house at different times, and also old broken glass-fronted cases, some of which still contained the remains of stuffed birds. We often used to play in these shippens. At other times we would climb the ladder to the hay loft and sit at the far end, where there was a door at first floor level. Through the chinks around the edge of this the sunlight entered, and it seemed as though there were living, dancing, golden sunbeams as the dust and chaff we stirred up moved slowly into the beam of light coming in round the door.

The guest house was more up-to-date than the farmhouse in that it had electricity, mains water and drainage. Nearby, in the corner of the field nearest to the house, just behind the barn, was the cesspool. There was no modern enclosed septic tank at that time. I do not remember that its grey sludge gave off much smell, but we were very fond of playing beside it, and probably poked the sludge with sticks culled from the nearby hedge. If we didn't poke it, then we threw stones into it that slowly sank out of sight.

Children generally are fascinated by smelly things and we were no exception. Beside one of the shippens was a disused stone trough filled with what we thought was the most delicious green stagnant water; it stank to high heaven. I can smell it now!

Apart from ourselves, Doris and her mother, there were two other people living at Moor View. Mr and Mrs Brailsford occupied the sitting room on the other side of the hall from us. We used to like visiting them as Mr Brailsford would swing us up into the air so that our heads nearly touched the ceiling. I remember going to tea with them once. Our bread and butter was cut up into fingers and built on our plates criss-crosswise into a tower, down the middle of which golden syrup was poured from a spoon. We then ate the sticky mess, though how we did this I cannot recall. Probably we were given a spoon. No grownup before or since had ever done that for us.

Most of the properties on this stretch of road were bungalows, sited on the west side; there were about ten in all, with just three more on the opposite side nearest to the moor. Most of the properties stood on large plots of ground. This little group comprised Vale Down; it was like a hamlet in itself as it was about 1½ miles from the centre of Lydford village and 2½ miles from Bridestowe. It is very little altered now from how it was when we lived there some sixty years ago.

On our side of the road was a wide piece of wasteland between the garden hedges of the houses and the road. Nowadays many of the properties have exercised squatters' rights on the waste outside and have taken it into their gardens. On the waste grew tall gorse bushes and brambles where in season Mother would gather the blackberries to make jam or jelly. Also growing there were plants of which I have only learned the name many years later; they had tall stems, mottled rather like rhubarb, and we used to call them rhubarb trees. It was *Polygonum cuspidatum* or, to give it its more familiar name, the dreaded Japanese Knotweed. For some reason it did not seem to spread rapidly in the way that it does nowadays. We could go in under them as they were taller than us. We often used to play on this waste where we had imaginary gardens. Mine was on the left-hand side as you went towards the gate of Moor View, and Diana's was on the right. We would sometimes make houses by spreading a shawl over the tops of nearby gorse bushes. All these years afterwards the scent of gorse in bloom immediately brings back to me the vision of a small boy of five, stretched out on the ground with the gorse bushes rising all round on three sides, a white lacy woollen shawl spread over the top through which the sunshine filtered, blue sky, and the all-pervading scent of the gorse flowers around us, engulfing us, wafting us off into a drowsy inactivity where time stood still.

Outside Moor View was a letterbox standing on a base of stones cemented together. By persistent wiggling of the stones, or hitting them with others, we managed to dislodge quite a few, although the pillar box was in no danger of falling down. The snapshot of Moor View on page 21 shows clearly the vandalised letterbox in the foreground. Another of our 'charming' tricks was to pour water from a small child's teapot into the letterbox itself.

We weren't the only children living on Vale Down at the time. There were two others: Keith Anderson, who was our own age and lived next door at Bray Tor; and Susan Dennis, who was a year or two older, and lived at Rookery Nook opposite us. We often used to play together although Susan and her mother did not come to live on Vale Down until after we had been there for some time.

Keith and his mother (there were no fathers as they were all away serving in the war) lived in an isolated bungalow built largely of corrugated iron; it was as primitive as our Cabin in that it had no mains water, electricity or drainage. Water was from a well behind the bungalow and the toilet was an earth closet. It was surrounded by trees and Keith's mother had one or two nasty shocks at night when she saw a dark face peering in at her windows. There were a large number of American troops camped not far away at Bridestowe and Willsworthy, some of whom were black.

There were also German prisoners of war at the same camps who were guarded by our soldiers and sometimes one would be allowed out, presumably under supervision, to come up and do some gardening at Moor View. I don't remember speaking to them; we just used to stand and watch them at work. Keith's mother had some form of protection, however, in the shape of a very fierce dog called Mickey or Mickey Mouse. He was a brown and white mongrel. The first time I went to visit them, soon after we moved to Moor View, I went alone and Mickey chased me up the lane and bit my bottom. I ran home to Mother, screeching. Thereafter, when it was known that we were coming, Mickey would be kept locked up until after we had arrived, by which time he was friendly.

On one occasion Diana nearly picked up an adder that was basking in the sun on the roadside waste outside the gate of Bray Tor. She thought it was a piece of string; fortunately, as she bent to pick it up, it vanished down a nearby hole. Mrs Anderson was quickly on the scene and with the aid of a spade hacked at the beginning of the hole, but the adder by then was well out of reach. We were certainly more wary thereafter.

Although we lived in a rural farming community, I don't think that we were very closely bound up with it. We were more in the nature of onlookers. On thinking back to those times, one thing that strikes me is that we never had any friends amongst the indigenous village children. Some of the farmers had land girls to help them out, and we were generally present at potato and corn harvests, though were too small to help.

Tom Kennard had an old-fashioned binder, which was pulled by one or two horses. On one side it had a flail, which revolved and cut the corn, which was then taken on a moving belt and bound with twine in the internal mechanism of the machine and thrown out as a sheaf through a chute on the other side. Later the sheaves would be stacked to form stooks.

In peacetime many of the fields were left fallow because the soil, being on the edge of the moor, was acid and poor, quite apart from being extremely stony and shallow. It needed frequent doses of lime and we would often see piles of it left lying about in the fields. However, under wartime regulations, they had to be ploughed up and planted, with what success I cannot say. Included in this ploughing was a part of the moor beside Vale Down, which I imagine had never been put under the plough before. Presumably this was too barren, as I don't recollect that the attempt to produce a crop on it was repeated. For refreshment, those working in the fields would usually bring with them cold tea in an old lemonade bottle. At harvest time I can remember being brought hot tea, from one of the bungalows near to the field where the harvesters were working; it was the sweetest drink I can ever remember, which seems strange in view of the wartime rationing of sugar.

Downtown Farm had venville rights and thus Tom Kennard kept a considerable number of sheep on the moor. They were all marked with a big letter K on their wool on one side, a practice which still continues. All the sheep had to be dipped, so were rounded up each year for this purpose. The sheep dip was in the first field off the bottom of the Cabin lane. Outside this field the lane widened out a little and had a gate at both ends, which when shut formed a small pound. Here the sheep would be tightly penned in until the time came for them to be dipped. We used to think it was rather cruel.

The dip was a concrete trough, about four feet deep and ten feet long; it had a wooden fence on the long sides to prevent the sheep getting out. They were pushed in at one end and, as they swam towards the other end, they were totally submerged by being pushed under with a prod wielded by the farmer or one of his men standing on the raised side. Exactly the same method is still used. Sometimes we watched the sheep being shorn. This would take place in one of the barns at the farm itself, or just outside it. The sheep for shearing were kept penned up in the farmyard. The shearing was all done by hand; the shearer held the sheep close to him, sideways on, and the fleece was then quickly cut off with the hand shears.

Some of the sheep were pastured in a field known as the Brake, on the edge of High Down. This consisted mostly of gorse bushes and was a good place for rabbits. (It was called the Brake because it was supposedly in the process of being broken in, or reclaimed, from the moor, although, in practice, this was not happening.) Nowadays the Brake has been thrown into the adjoining field and consists of just grass, so is no different from the rest of the farm.

A large part of High Down was enclosed within stone walls and this, although otherwise indistinguishable from the open moor in its vegetation, was known as the Newtake – only we never knew it as that. In the dialect, it was always referred to as the Noodick, and sheep were pastured here. At that time much of the Newtake was covered with heather, and harebells grew plentifully together with foxgloves. It has since been 'improved' and now has little else but grass growing there. Certainly the harebells have long since been destroyed.

One of the quaint ideas held by old Mrs Kennard, which Mother told me about, was that one should never go out of doors without wearing a hat, because nits dropped from the trees and if you didn't wear one then you would get nits in your hair!

Sometimes we would see tramps walking the roads, or they would come knocking at the back door of Moor View, begging for food or perhaps for work. At a somewhat later date (after the war) a tramp lived for a considerable time in the lane leading up to the Cabin.

On our infrequent excursions to Okehampton, we would see gypsies camped on the roadside verges of Sourton Moor. My sister had a book about gypsies featuring a donkey called Pompey, so to see them in real life added interest to the story. The ones on Sourton Down were real gypsies of course, not the travellers one hears about nowadays. Another frequently seen object on the road at Sourton was a working steamroller.

With all the Camps in the neighbourhood and the military training areas, the roads were often busy with convoys of army lorries carrying troops or towing guns. Very often if American troops were in the lorries they would throw out packets of chewing gum for us children. I remember going to a children's party given by the American troops at Bridestowe and eating circular ring doughnuts – something I had not had before.

In Lydford there were quite a number of families like ourselves, who had come from larger centres of population to escape the Blitz. They, and the troops, must have added much to the social life of the village. It must have seemed very quiet again after the war when all these 'vurriners' left. Village life was never quite the same.

Dartmoor had been 'discovered' in Victorian times and many private hotels and guest houses had sprung up to cater for the visitors. One suspects that whilst a few people still go to stay on the moor for their holiday and enjoy walking on it, the majority of its hotels and guest houses are now used by people with cars who find them a pleasant central setting from which to go off each day to the coasts of Devon and Cornwall, or the cities of Exeter or Plymouth, hardly setting foot on the moor proper during the whole of their stay. Times have changed; the old walking-type of visitor was still much in evidence at the time about which I write. In any event few people had cars then. Whilst far more people than ever walk on the moors now, most of them travel by car from the towns and cities of Devon and so generally do not stay, but return home again after their walk.

I mentioned earlier that Doris had a prewar Austin Seven, and we would occasionally get a ride with her to market at either Tavistock or Okehampton. In common with all other cars in wartime, its headlights were fitted with a black visor with small horizontal slits to allow only a minimal amount of light through. She eventually disposed of the car a few years after the war ended, as one of the wheels came off when she was driving down into Lydford village.

All Doris's brothers and sisters were farmers or farmers' wives living within a few miles; sometimes we used to go with her to visit them. Petrol was rationed, so there was little opportunity for pleasure motoring. Two of her sisters lived at Chillaton, a brother farmed at Bridestowe, and her eldest brother lived at Highhampton. One of her nieces taught us two of the songs popular at that time: 'You Are My Sunshine' and 'Underneath The Lantern' ('Lilli Marlene'). In our sitting room was an instrument known as a Dulcitone, which must have contained tubular bars; it had a sound rather like a celesta. Father taught us to play another popular song on this, 'Run Rabbit Run'. Naturally, we only played with one finger. Also in our room was a harmonium, the pedals of which we would pump up and down, but fortunately for the rest of the people in the house, the keyboard was too high for us to reach, or else was kept locked, so we were never able to serenade anyone. Keith and his mother had an old portable wind-up gramophone which we used to play a great deal, and also a radio that worked off an accumulator.

The Cult of Fairies

It may seem strange that in Dartmoor country I should start writing about fairies rather than the indigenous species known as pixies. However, in all the time we lived at Lydford I cannot recall ever hearing any mention of the latter. Years later when I asked Mother about this, she said the only time she could recall hearing anything about them was at a Women's Institute meeting in the village when Mrs Radford, who was the Lady of the Manor living at Ingo Brake, gave a talk in which she said that she believed in pixies as her washing had once been taken by them. However, Susan Dennis encouraged us in a very strong belief in fairies. She had a book with 'pop-up' pictures and one of them consisted of a house with a sheet of cellophane inside it. On this was reflected a picture of a fairy, which seemed to be floating about in the air in the house. She also encouraged us to study the pansies which grew in the garden of Moor View. We were told to look at the hole in the centre from which the stamens grew. Susan suggested that this was where the fairies lived. We looked and looked, but all in vain, though our belief did not falter.

At other times she would get us to peer along the back of the woodshed which stood adjacent to, but not touching, the hedge between Moor View and the adjoining house. Very tall sycamore trees grew on top of this hedge. As we looked down the somewhat dark gap between the back of the buildings and the hedge, Susan told us that the Fairy Queen had just vanished out of sight at the other end of the buildings. Again we were disappointed in that we never saw the Fairy Queen, but this did not stop us looking from time to time, always expecting that one day we would glimpse the Queen. We were always convinced that we had only just missed her.

On another occasion Susan came close to persuading Diana that if she met her in the garden of Rookery Nook at midnight, the fairies would be there to play with and they would have the most marvellous fairground; she described to Diana in some detail the swings and roundabouts and slides. Diana never went to find out. I expect she was asleep and anyway Mother, who slept in the same room with us, would never have let her get up at that time of night to go out. Susan would not have been there either!

About a mile from Moor View in the Okehampton direction, and not far beyond the Fox and Hounds, but on the other side, was a small wood beside the main road. This grew near a tiny house which Grandfather had once thought of buying, before he had the Cabin built. It was a one room up and one room down dwelling and we called it the Salt Cellar. It was demolished many years ago. We sometimes went to this wood and there we would make houses for the fairies to live in. Part of the wood had been cut down many years previously; the stumps of the felled trees had partly rotted away and were covered with moss. It was on these stumps that we used to make our houses for the fairies with bits of moss and bark and the odd bit of lichen. Sometimes we found the red 'Fairies Cap' lichen growing and would put a bit of this in our house. I suppose that in such a rural setting, supposedly the natural habitat of fairies, it is easier to believe in them. Susan Dennis must have had a vivid imagination, but then again, so did we.

With beauty all around us on every side, we did not need much in the way of toys. A child's imagination is a wonderful thing. I wonder if today's children, who are under constant pressure to grow up, are missing an infinitely precious part of childhood; they so often have to be amused by artificial stimuli and sometimes seem to be incapable of amusing themselves.

Neighbours

A few houses below us lived the two Misses Bate in a property called Bracken. This was the last house on Vale Down in the direction of Lydford. One of them was obviously a bit feeble of mind and was cared for by the other sister. Once she nearly caused an accident by darting out from a field gate onto the main road with a bunch of wild flowers for Mother, who was, in turn, hurtling steeply down towards her on her bicycle with Diana perched on the back. Fortunately, in taking swift evasive action, Mother managed not only to stay on her bike but also to avoid running over Miss Bate.

This bicycle was our only means of transport. It had a carrier on the back over the mudguard on which one of us could sit with our legs resting on footrests screwed to the rear forks. Sometimes we both managed to sit on the carrier. The bicycle had the old type of 28-inch wheels and no gears.

The other Miss Bate, who was perfectly normal, owned a car which, even to us, seemed antiquated. A Standard from the early 1920s, it was very high off the ground (or so it seemed to us little ones), with a battery on the running board and a step that had to be let down before you could climb into the back. Very occasionally we would be taken for a ride in it, probably only for a couple of miles or so – perhaps up onto High Down by the Lyd.

Next door to the Misses Bate lived Mr and Mrs Goodson at Ridgemoor, whom we visited sometimes, but of whom I can recall nothing special. Further along the main road, but towards the Dartmoor Inn, the Miltons lived at Elim with their sons, whom we knew slightly.

In the other direction, two doors beyond Mrs Anderson and Keith, Mr and Mrs Millman lived in a wooden white-painted bungalow called Sunset Cottage. In this they had a cuckoo clock and we liked to go to see them and watch the cuckoo fly out of his door, especially at midday. We were fascinated by this clock. No one else in our experience had one and I rather think I would have liked to have got my hands on it to find out what made it go cuckoo! Mrs Millman gave us odd scraps of varicoloured material with which we played. We do not seem to have had much else to do with the other people who lived on Vale Down.

I remember that there was a lady living a bit further up Vale Down who accidentally ate some weedkiller. (Or was it she drank some lavatory cleanser?) We were most interested to learn that it had burnt her insides. Children like macabre and gory details and we learned this bit of information from hearing grownups talking. It was the phrase about her inside being 'burnt up' which made the story stick in my mind. Whether she lived or died I cannot recall and I do not think we knew her. Next to her bungalow was a house called Telde, where Mr and Mrs Summers lived with their daughter, Dell. Mr Summers was the manager of the Peat Works in the Rattlebrook valley, which at that time was in one of its sporadic periods of production.

Next to Telde was Arms Tor House, which was also a guest house; here some of our relations or friends would occasionally stay when coming to visit us. Beyond this was just one more house, Burley View, and then the open moor known as Fernworthy Down, which at that time was unimproved land. Sometimes, for one of our walks, we would go over a stile beside this last house and walk over Fernworthy (locally pronounced 'Vinnery') Down to the railway line, which we would cross and then continue across more downland and lanes to get to Lydford village. I remember that towards the end of this route there were the rusting remains of an old car in the lane.

Miscellaneous Memories

After I commenced school, Mother, who was a trained teacher, began to teach at Mary Tavy Village School. This was about six miles away and involved a long and arduous daily cycle journey climbing up the hill to Black Down and down the other side to Mary Tavy. And this was with Diana riding pillion! She was too young at this stage to go to school.

From the bridge over the River Lyd to the first level part of Black Down must be about a mile of steady ascent, and her bicycle had no gears to make life a little easier. What it must have been like in wet weather I don't know; Black Down is very exposed and the road over it in places is over 1,000 feet above sea level. On the way there, if it was wet, she would have been riding into the teeth of the prevailing wind and must have arrived at school thoroughly drenched.

On the return journey there was another long ascent to be made from Mary Tavy up to Black Down, and along the road beside Gibbet Hill. It was here, long ago, that criminals were supposed to have been hanged.

Mother's teaching at Mary Tavy came to an abrupt end when Diana caught measles.

As children, we were very interested in the mining remains at Mary Tavy, which had once been the centre of rich and important copper mines. There were holes in the ground that were the remains of old shafts and also the ruins of brick calciners where arsenic was refined as a by-product. Of course I did not know what these remains were at the time – this knowledge was gained later.

Scattered about beside the rivers Lyd and Doe are many relics of former, mostly opencast, tin mining, with heaps of spoil left behind by the mediaeval tin streamers and later miners. There are also the ruins of a few small buildings connected with the mining. There were three in our neighbourhood. The most interesting of these was at Dick's Well Pits in the Doe valley, behind Widgery Cross. It is a most beautiful spot, which looks across to the range comprising Rattlebrook Hill, Sharp and Hare Tors. The terrain consisted

Fording Bridge

of scattered surface granite, interspersed with (in those days) much heather and whortleberry plants. It is marked on the Ordnance Survey map as Foxhole Mine, but we never knew it by this name. In fact, Dick's Well Pits are the enormous and deep excavations further up the valley.

Dick's Well Pits

In front of the cottage are the remains of two circular buddles with the miners' spring in between. Nearby is a leat, now dry, with an embankment on the higher ground, which took water via a wooden launder to a wheel. The remains of the wheel pit are still clearly visible and the walls of the two-roomed cottage, with a fireplace in each room, still stand to a considerable height. Unlike Bleak House, it does not seem to have deteriorated with the passage of time since I first knew it.

We visited Dick's Well Pits in the whortleberry season to pick the worts. On another occasion we went there with my Grandfather Chown and several young friends from the village (the Jolliffes mentioned later). One of these dug around in the turf outside the cottage in an endeavour to discover what the roof material had been. He said he found a piece of slate, so the roof must have been slated. However, I think this is improbable; it was much more likely to have been thatched.

Further out into the moor ('out auver', as they say in the dialect) was an extensive peatworks which was worked sporadically throughout the war and for a few years afterwards, although I do not think it was ever regarded as a successful commercial venture. This was the site of Bleak House mentioned earlier. In former times they had been reached by a narrow gauge railway, which joined the main Southern line at Bridestowe station, but this had all been dismantled before the time of which I write. Mother used to tell us how she had ridden back to Bridestowe on one of the trucks of this railway when she was a young girl. Sometimes we would walk part way along the former trackbed, where many of the sleepers were still in place, but, for one reason or another, we never made it all the way to the peatworks.

What a picturesque station Bridestowe used to be with its oil lamps. On one side, where the ground rose steeply, the banks were completely covered with dense rhododendron bushes, which formed a thick hedge rising from the back of the platform on the 'down' side. The road leading down to the station from the Fox and Hounds had a magnificent avenue of beech trees, which arched overhead like the vaulting of some great cathedral. On one side of the

Widgery Cross

road, under the trees, is a verge that was used as an ammunition store, presumably because it was completely hidden from the air by the trees overhead. There were corrugated iron stores, rather like small Nissen huts, and before you could walk or drive down the road you had to produce your identity card to the guard on duty. There was another guard at the lower end. At the top of this road was a house with a large bell hanging out on a cradle from the first floor. This was painted red, and was supposed to have been put there by a nervous owner of the house who was afraid of being robbed. I never heard it rung.

We could pick up lengths of silver paper on the moor. These had been put there, so I was told, as decoys, so that in the moonlight the German bombers would see them glinting and think they were over a town and so drop their bombs where they could do no harm to the population. Whether this was true or not I cannot say, but at any rate no bombs were ever dropped as a result. However, a plane crashed on the down near the Fox and Hounds and we could pick up small pieces of wreckage. Plymouth took a pounding in the Blitz and every night there was a mass exodus from the city into the surrounding countryside. Mother said that she was able to see the reflection of the flames in the night sky as the city burned.

28

From High Down above the River Lyd, in the distance we could see the protecting barrage balloons over the city and the River Tamar. One of them was involved in a bizarre incident. On Monday, 22 July 1940, a German pilot by the alliterative name of Hauptmann Hajo Hermann, in trying to avoid such a balloon, actually stalled his engine on top of it. With unbelievable good fortune, he was able to regain control of his Junkers Ju 88 after falling off the balloon upside-down.

Meanwhile, away from all this pandemonium, under a small group of pine trees in the garden of Moor View was a small shallow pit, dug for use as a shelter if the bombers came. Fortunately it was never needed.

The water supply for Bridestowe and Vale Down came from a small spring in a fenced-in boggy intake on the col between Arms Tor and Widgery Cross. Owing to the presence of so many troops in their camp at Bridestowe, sometimes this used to fail altogether as the demand exceeded the supply. For this reason Doris had the old pump at Moor View put back into working order.

Incidentally, my grandfather Chown was one of those people who had the ability to 'dowse': that is, he was a water diviner. I well remember him cutting a forked hazel twig from a hedge near which were some springs, and how it swung violently when he held it out in front of him. When I tried it nothing happened, but, when he put his hands over mine, the twig turned so that it was impossible to hold it and I had to let go.

Schooldays

During our stay at Lydford the time came for me to start school. I had previously been to two or three nursery schools in Exmouth, but the thought of going to the village school at Lydford definitely did not appeal to me. When the day duly arrived, whilst clinging to the iron rails of my mother's bedstead, I indulged in a prolonged fit of screaming, thinking that this would ensure that I was not sent. It was all to no avail and off to school I went.

Originally built in 1878 to accommodate up to ninety children, the school was down in the village and stood in the middle of an asphalted playground completely surrounded by it. The infants' classroom was at the back, with a larger room or hall at the front where the older children met. There were entrance lobbies on both sides, in one of which was a dolls' house. The toilets were at the side and you had to go outdoors to reach them. There seemed to be quite a large number of children at the school when I went there, the numbers having been swollen by the arrival of evacuees. The older girls used the playground on one side of the buildings, whilst the older boys used the other side. We younger children used the part of the playground that was in front of the school. Classes, however, were mixed. When the bell was rung at the end of playtime, we had to line up in our classes in front of the main wall before walking in order back into the classroom.

There were only two teachers: Mrs Mitchell, the headmistress, who lived in the schoolhouse next door and taught the junior school, and Miss Gale, who taught me and the other infants. I seem to remember that she was kind but firm, but very little of what I learned remains with me. Miss Gale had a cat that produced kittens; Doris had one of them, which she called Fluffy.

On the back of our classroom door there hung a picture frame and each week the coloured picture in it would be changed. We all had to close our eyes at this point and were not permitted to open them until the picture had been changed. We did raffia work and I made a teapot stand, weaving the white and orange raffia round and round the cardboard frame and over and under the weft. A display of work was put on in the Nicholls Hall in the village and my mat was one of the items shown and I was very proud of it. It was used by my grandmother Chown for several years afterwards. It never really wore out – the raffia just became so stained with tea that it looked disreputable. Also at the display I remember string bags being shown. These I think were made by Miss Gale knotting string together like a fishing net, commencing at a nail driven into the back of the classroom door or into a wall. Mother had one of these bags, which she used for shopping; they had a considerable capacity, as the string expanded as more items were put in.

Mother also did her bit for our education. As we were isolated, she taught us both to knit at a very early age. She also set arithmetic problems for us to do and encouraged us in our reading skills. After a while Diana became old enough to join me at Lydford School.

Sometimes we would go into the big classroom for *Music and Movement* programmes, which were relayed on the radio. I enjoyed these very much and we would also listen to them at home. I was always sorry when they were over. I was quite carried away by the words and pictures conjured up by the little stories and the accompanying music. The love of music was obviously within me: later on I learned to play the piano, and in my late teens progressed to the church organ.

My education wasn't confined to the four walls of the classroom. I well recall a nature ramble down a lane to part of the River Lyd, which was close to the village where Lydford Mill had once been. The lane passed under a large viaduct carrying the railway line to Lydford Junction Station and on to Plymouth. A little further up the river is the delightful spot called Kitt's Steps or Skit's Steps. This waterfall was reached by an unsurfaced country lane. I suppose we were meant to identify the different flowers we saw along the way, but all I can remember seeing are cornflowers and campions. On another occasion we must have found a caterpillar, as I remember it being kept in a jar filled with leaves on a windowsill of our classroom.

Other memories of wildlife at Lydford are of the tremendous number of slugs, which would appear as soon as there was any wet or damp weather; with a generous supply of rainfall, this was often. Frequently on our family walks we saw butterflies and Mother told us their names, together with those of the wild flowers we encountered. Sloes were also plentiful in season.

The school had its own garden next to the Police House. Here we used to do our own bit of 'digging for Victory'. Different classes were allotted patches of garden. All I can remember growing were Sweet Williams which, obviously, would not have done much for the war food production effort.

Gas mask drill was another part of school and home life. Ours were shaped like Mickey Mouse and we had to put them on, making sure that they were a tight fit round the face, and then practise breathing through them. On another occasion the Army put on some sort of display in the village street outside the Nicholls Hall. We went to this from school and they demonstrated an inflatable rubber dinghy. Some of the more fortunate children were allowed to sit in it and were shown how to fasten themselves in so as to shut out the water and keep themselves dry.

Often we walked to school with Mrs Anderson and Keith. He did not go to the village school, but to a private one at Bridge House on the far side of Lydford Bridge, which spans the Gorge. Mrs Anderson was in the process of writing a children's story and to pass the time on the walk each day she would give us an instalment.

Whilst it is generally true that it is only the sunny days one remembers from childhood, I have a recollection of walking to school in the rain and seeing all the colours of the rainbow reflected in the puddles on the road. This was caused by petrol spilt by the army vehicles and tanks using it.

We had a sports day, which was held in a field just up the hill from the school, near to the railway line. The races included egg and spoon, three-legged and wheelbarrow. I did not stay to school dinners (which in any event I think were not provided) but went to lunch with the Joliffes, an evacuee family from London living on the outskirts of the village in a wooden bungalow called Fairfield. Sometimes we had a bath there. Their children were our age and we used to play together. Almost opposite Fairfield was another bungalow called Horsefield, where Mrs Coxe and her daughter Susannah lived. She was about our age too and we were friends.

Some children brought food with them to school and in winter if they had a pasty this would be placed on top of the coke stove in the front classroom to heat up in time for dinner. Sometimes I would take some of Mother's blackberry jelly in a Bakelite beaker for lunch.

There was one boy who was older than me and bullied me. On more than one occasion he took my chocolate. Eventually we somehow brokered an agreement. Most days, I had an apple to eat. When I had eaten it, I used to pass him the core,which he would ravenously devour. This worked very well; I didn't like apple cores and would only have thrown them away. Looking back one suspects that perhaps he was not fed properly at home, so that his bullying was caused by hunger. He was a farmer's son and gave the impression of being very poor, and I remember that he had problems of personal hygiene. As soon as sowing or harvesting time came round, he, and other members of his family, would be absent from school. Their parents kept them home to work on the farm. This was not allowed, but nothing seemed to be done about it, although it was well known why they were away.

A Dartmoor Boyhood

Each day, when school was over, we caught a bus home from the War Memorial. Towards the end of my time at the school, the bus no longer came into the village, so we had to walk about a mile up the road to the Dartmoor Inn to catch it from there.

Some memories fade, but others burn bright, sometimes for the wrong reasons.

I can vividly remember being read or told the Chandler Harris stories of Brer Rabbit and Brer Fox and also learning short division. Although I mastered this we must have gone on to something else or had a holiday, because when we came back to doing it again I found I had forgotten the technique. Fortunately we used the same problem sums and I copied out the ones I had done previously, which were several pages back in my exercise book. Inevitably, this meant that all those previously solved wrongly were still wrong. We had just about reached the end of this supply and were about to reach new sums when I left the school for good and returned to Exmouth. I was extremely relieved – it was in the nick of time! What could I have said to Miss Gale, one moment apparently being able to do short division and the next not having the faintest notion! I wonder if she saw through me? It doesn't seem to have crossed my mind then that I could have simply asked Mother, a trained teacher, how to do short division. She was always keen for us to learn and make progress.

And so we left Vale Down and returned to Exmouth for good just before the end of the war. I see from the school register that this was on 3 March 1944. The reason was that Grandmother Chown had stood on a chair in the bay window of her home to look down the road to see if American troops were going to be billeted on her sister. (She lived further down the road, on the opposite side.) The chair slipped on the polished lino and she fell heavily and broke her thigh. This resulted in an extended stay in hospital. Therefore Mother had to return to help look after her and grandfather, who was out on business during the day.

Our time on Dartmoor was an extraordinarily happy one, despite the war, of which I suppose we were only dimly aware. Looking back on our childhood it seems to have been idyllic, and so it must have been, because Mother also always spoke of it with such great affection.

My last recollection of my village childhood is of the Victory Bonfire. (Perhaps we had already left the village by this time and were back on holiday staying at Moor View, as we did almost every year for quite a bit more of our childhood.) This was built near the crossroads behind the War Memorial on a triangular piece of ground. To us it seemed a huge structure, towering into the air. It was built crisscross fashion, like the bread-and-butter fingers mentioned earlier. Before going down to see it lit, Mother and Doris went up to the Fox and Hounds for a celebration drink.

Doetor Falls

The bonfire was followed by dancing in the Nicholls Hall. Mother remembered that 'Spanny' Palmer, a local character, got drunk; whilst the bonfire was burning, he was swinging a dead rabbit round and round his head!

With the flames of the Victory bonfire burning bright, it seems an appropriate point to say farewell to my Dartmoor childhood. One part of my experience of childhood thus vanished for ever as the flames and smoke spiralled up into the night sky. The physical experiences have gone, but the memories still linger on just as fresh, clear and fragrant to me all these years later. It's as though they had happened yesterday.

Postscript

After the war ended we still used to holiday at Lydford almost every year. Occasionally we would stay at the Cabin, but more often we'd stay with Doris Crocker at Moor View. In 1953 I stayed at the Cabin with a school friend and for some years thereafter with other friends, even being there on my own occasionally.

In the late 1950s Tom Kennard was forced to sell Downtown Farm and the new owners made various changes, chief of which was the total felling of the trees in the field hedges. They then layered them. The privacy that we had enjoyed was gone to a certain extent, and whilst in the Kennards' time nothing other than sheep or ponies were kept in the Cabin field, the new farmer often had cattle there. These trampled the grass all round the Cabin and rubbed themselves against it. In one year the field was actually ploughed.

Unfortunately the beauty and magic that had been there were destroyed. The gorse bushes had disappeared and thus the dew diamonds glittering in the sun were also gone for ever. A stone trough was inserted in the bottom of the pool in front of the pipe carrying the spring water from the ground, which made getting a jug under it to fill the watercan that much more difficult.

I think the last holiday I spent at the Cabin was in 1960. In the very severe winter of 1962–1963, the Cabin was buried under a huge snowdrift and severely damaged. A large hole appeared in the roof of the bedroom hut and the kitchen hut had become partially detached. In addition, the wood of the kitchen hut was beginning to rot away after exposure to so many harsh winters. With the remote likelihood of any members of the family wanting to stay there, it was demolished and the remains disposed of… but the memories live on!

A Dartmoor Boyhood